border to border · teen to teen · border to border · teen to teen · border to border

TEENS IN VENEZUELA

Teens in Venezuela

Venezuela

by Sandy Donovan and
Caryn Gracey Jones

Content Adviser: Ines Rojas, M.A.,
Assistant Professor, School of Modern Languages,
Universidad de Los Andes, Venezuela

Reading Adviser: Katie Van Sluys, Ph.D.,
Department of Teacher Education,
DePaul University

Compass Point Books ✦ Minneapolis, Minnesota

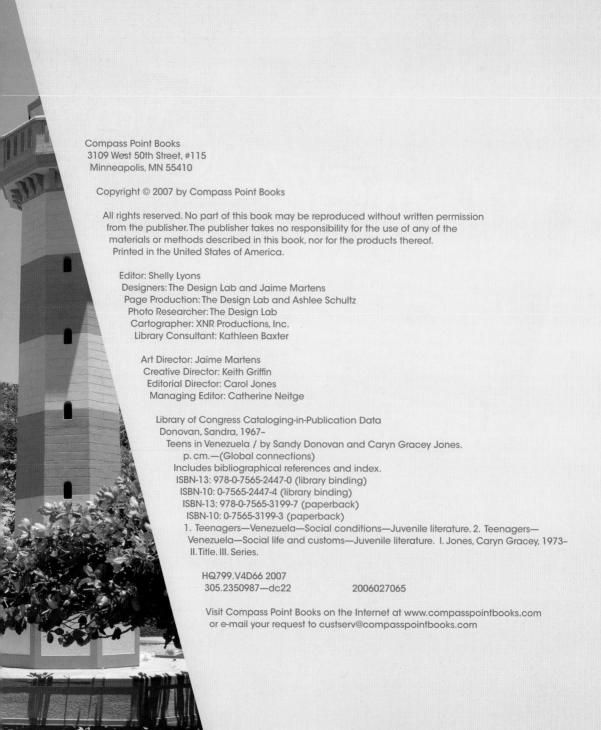

Compass Point Books
3109 West 50th Street, #115
Minneapolis, MN 55410

Editor: Shelly Lyons
Designers: The Design Lab and Jaime Martens
Page Production: The Design Lab and Ashlee Schultz
Photo Researcher: The Design Lab
Cartographer: XNR Productions, Inc.
Library Consultant: Kathleen Baxter

Art Director: Jaime Martens
Creative Director: Keith Griffin
Editorial Director: Carol Jones
Managing Editor: Catherine Neitge

Library of Congress Cataloging-in-Publication Data
Donovan, Sandra, 1967–
  Teens in Venezuela / by Sandy Donovan and Caryn Gracey Jones.
    p. cm.—(Global connections)
  Includes bibliographical references and index.
  ISBN-13: 978-0-7565-2447-0 (library binding)
  ISBN-10: 0-7565-2447-4 (library binding)
  ISBN-13: 978-0-7565-3199-7 (paperback)
  ISBN-10: 0-7565-3199-3 (paperback)
  1. Teenagers—Venezuela—Social conditions—Juvenile literature. 2. Teenagers—
  Venezuela—Social life and customs—Juvenile literature. I. Jones, Caryn Gracey, 1973–
  II. Title. III. Series.

    HQ799.V4D66 2007
    305.2350987—dc22   2006027065

Visit Compass Point Books on the Internet at www.compasspointbooks.com
  or e-mail your request to custserv@compasspointbooks.com

Table of Contents

Caracas

MEXICO

Rio Grande

Gulf of Mexico

THE BAHAMAS

CUBA

BELIZE

GUATEMALA

HONDURAS

JAMAICA

EL SALVADOR

NICARAGUA

DOM. REP.

COSTA RICA

Caribbean Sea

PANAMA

VENEZUELA

COLOMBIA

GUYANA

FRENCH GUIANA

SURINAME

ECUADOR

Negro

Amazon

Madeira

PERU

BRAZIL

BOLIVIA

PARAGUAY

CHILE

Parana

ARGENTINA

Missouri

Colorado

L. Winnipeg

ATLANTIC
OCEAN

Mediterranean Sea

Rhine

Red Sea

Nile

Niger

L. Chad

Congo

IRELAND
U.K.
NETH.
BELGIUM LUX.
GERMANY
CZECH
SLOVAKIA
ROMANIA
SWITZERLAND
AUSTRIA
HUNGARY
BULGARIA
TURKEY
FRANCE
ITALY
GREECE
SYRIA IRAQ
ANDORRA
LEBANON
ISRAEL
SAUDI
ARABIA
PORTUGAL
SPAIN
TUNISIA
EGYPT
MOROCCO
LIBYA
ALGERIA
Canary Islands
WESTERN SAHARA
MALI
NIGER
CHAD
MAURITANIA
SENEGAL
BURKINA
NIGERIA
GAMBIA
BENIN
CAMEROON
CONGO
GUINEA BISSAU GUINEA
TOGO
SIERRA LEONE
IVORY COAST
GHANA
EQUATORIAL GUINEA
CONGO
LIBERIA
SAO TOME & PRINCIPE
GABON
ANGOLA

TEENS IN VENEZUELA

VENEZUELA IS A NATION OF CONTRASTS. IT SPANS COASTAL AREAS, FERTILE PLAINS, MOUNTAINS, AND RAIN FORESTS. IT INCLUDES COSMOPOLITAN CITIES AND ONE OF THE WORLD'S MOST PRIMITIVE INDIAN TRIBES. During the 1970s—thanks to immense profits reaped from oil sales—Venezuela was one of South America's richest countries. But today almost half of its 25.7 million citizens live in extreme poverty. This contrast is particularly evident in the cities, where some teens live in steel-and-glass high-rise apartment buildings and others crowd into one-room dwellings with their extended families.

Teens make up approximately 35 percent of the country's population. There are varying lifestyles among the teens in Venezuela. Some teens live in the Amazon rain forest, where the focus of their lives is survival and tradition. Other teens live in large cities, attend school, and go home to their apartments in the city. But throughout Venezuela, teens share their country's rich culture, geography, and history.

The Venezuelan government insists that every citizen be entitled to free education.

1

Focus on Education

"HOLA, CHAMO!"
"¿CÓMO ESTÁS?"

It's not quite 7 A.M. in Caracas, Venezuela's capital city, but already the streets are filled with the shouts of children and teenagers making their way to school. They call to each other in Spanish, the national language they share with most South Americans. But some of their slang, such as *chamo*, which means "friend," is uniquely Venezuelan. Dressed in uniforms of white shirts and navy blue pants or skirts, the students wait at public bus stops or walk together down the city's crowded sidewalks.

Arriving at school, groups of friends might head straight to the cafeteria and help themselves to cereal

chamo
CHAH-moh

or an *arepa,* a fried or grilled pancake filled with cheese or eggs. Some public schools that take part in the Venezuelan government's meal program serve free breakfast to students. Soon the students filter into their classrooms. Since the schools have no lockers, they carry their books with them in backpacks all day.

arepa
ah-RAY-pah

Monday through Friday, the school day consists of five to six 45-minute classes. In primary schools—for students from age 6 to about age 12—lessons include reading, writing, math, natural sciences such as biology and geography, and social sciences such as history and civics. In high school, students take on more complex subjects, based on the type of high school they attend.

A Typical High School Students' Daily Schedule

6 A.M. Wake up and wash; eat breakfast or get to school in time to eat before classes begin.

7 A.M. Walk or take a bus to school; rural students might ride a bike.

7:30 A.M. Classes begin in homeroom; classes last 45 minutes. In larger schools, students switch rooms for every class. In smaller schools, students stay in the same classroom all day.

1 P.M. Midday meal, the largest meal of the day; students might eat at school or at home.

2 P.M. Most schools are out for the day; students head home to begin homework or help around the house.

2–5 P.M Visit with friends, meet for sports practice, or help their parents do shopping and other errands.

8 P.M. Family dinnertime.

10:30-11 P.M. Bedtime.

Teen Scenes

In a wealthy neighborhood on the outskirts of Caracas, a 15-year-old girl wakes early in her pink-and-white decorated bedroom. A family servant has already prepared her breakfast of eggs, fruit, and cheese-filled arepas, and she pages through her history book as she eats. She has a full day ahead at her private Catholic high school, where she takes her studies seriously—she hopes to be accepted at one of Venezuela's top colleges and become a diplomat, like her father.

Meanwhile, in a neighborhood on the other side of Caracas, another 15-year-old also wakes early. It's still dark in the one-room house he shares with his parents, two brothers, and grandmother, and he hurries outside to use the outhouse. Rather than heading to school, he will spend the day on a crowded street, selling items his family has made, hoping to earn money to contribute to his family's small income.

Miles away in a small farming village, a 14-year-old boy is up early picking lemons and limes from neatly planted rows of citrus trees. By 7 A.M., he has already put in two hours of crop picking, and soon he will hop on his bicycle for the 45-minute ride to a technical high school. He is studying to be a medical technician, and he hopes to find a job in one of Venezuela's larger cities once he earns his degree.

These three distinctly different scenes are all uniquely Venezuelan. With people younger than 18 making up a larger portion of their nation's population than any other age group, Venezuelan teens understand that they are their country's future. Some are privileged enough to have the opportunity to go on to university. Some are needed at home to earn money to support their family. But all share a need to work hard to accomplish their dreams and improve their country.

As funding increases, the number of students attending school goes up, too.

At lunch, they gather in the cafeteria, if their school is large enough to have one, or they eat at desks in their class-rooms. Like breakfast, lunch is provided free of cost at some schools. Meals usually consist of arepas or *empanadas* (fried turnovers). The school day usually ends before 2 P.M., and students head home to study, help their parents with chores, and get together with friends.

empanadas
em-pah-NAH-das

High School Choice

High school is not required for Venezuelan teenagers. Those who do attend—about four-fifths of all teens—get to choose from three types of schools. Two-year technical high schools teach specific skills to prepare students for jobs such as electrician, computer programmer, nurse, or medical technician. Students who plan to go on to college may choose from two types of three-year high schools. One focuses on the sciences, and students who choose this program study biology, chemistry, physics, and math. These classes prepare them for careers as doctors, engineers, or pharmacists. The other high school focuses on the humanities. If they choose this program, they'll study languages such as Spanish and English, history, or political science. They can become teachers, lawyers, translators, or television and newspaper reporters.

Venezuela puts a high importance on education for everyone.

In the early 1980s, Venezuela's adult illiteracy rate was about 16 percent. By 2003, it had been reduced to just 6.6 percent.

Students in smaller cities and towns have similar school days. They wear the same uniforms as city students and study the same subjects, but their schools may be smaller—sometimes only one room—and they may have to travel farther to get there. Throughout Venezuela, the school year lasts from mid-September to mid-July.

Schools in Need

Venezuela's commitment to education is demonstrated by its literacy rate of more than 93 percent—the highest in South America. In fact, about 90 percent of Venezuelan children under the age of 14 attend school, and 80 percent continue on until they graduate from high school at age 18.

But that leaves one-fifth of teens in Venezuela who don't finish high school. Widespread poverty is the main reason for the dropouts. About 50 percent of Venezuelans earn an income below the poverty line, which is the income that the government estimates families need to support themselves. For families living below the poverty line, sending children to school may be difficult or impossible. Public school is free because it is funded by the government, but often children in low-income families need to earn money to help support the family. They may work on a farm, sell items on a city street, or even work in a factory instead of attending school.

Poverty affects education as much as it affects all other aspects of Venezuelan life. Children from low-income families usually have vastly different school experiences than children from middle- and upper-income families. For instance, poorer children are more likely to be in an overcrowded public school.

The need to support a family contributes to Venezuela's drop-out rate.

In 2006, there were 15 percent more girls than boys enrolled in secondary education.

It's not just families that suffer from a lack of money in Venezuela today. The government is often short of funds, too. With more Venezuelans under the age of 18 than in any other age group, the need for schools is great. The government does not have the money to repair many older school buildings, buy supplies such as books and computers, or hire enough teachers. The result is that often public school students end up sitting in crowded classrooms.

The best-equipped, least-crowded schools in Venezuela tend to be private schools sponsored by the Roman Catholic Church. Almost one-fifth of all students go to private school, and the majority of these students come from middle- and upper-income families. But the church does offer scholarships to help lower-income families pay tuition. Private school students often receive a better education than public school students. Not only do they usually have fewer children in a classroom, they also may have newer equipment and offer more subjects. For instance, most private schools start teaching

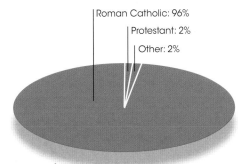

Religion in Venezuela

Roman Catholic: 96%

Protestant: 2%

Other: 2%

Source: United States Central Intelligence Agency.
The World Factbook—Venezuela.

Students walk to a public school in Caracas.

English at age 6, while public school students may not begin English classes until age 13 or 14.

Improvements Under Way

While it's true that many schools in Venezuela are in bad shape, the situation is getting better. Until a few years ago, many Venezuelans did not even go to school. At some public schools, parents had to pay tuition for their children's education. Many families couldn't pay, and as a result, in 1990, nearly 36 percent of all children left school before age 14. Another 13 percent did not finish high school.

In 1998, the Venezuelan government began a massive effort to improve education. Public schools were no longer allowed to charge tuition. Starting in 2000, with the help of the military, the government built more than 3,000 schools. A widespread media campaign featured television and radio announcements on the importance of education. By 2003, 21 percent more students were staying in school. This reflects the enhanced state of education in Venezuela, although there is still room for improvement in the public schools. Many families save their money so they can send their children to private schools, and almost all children from the wealthiest families attend private schools.

Government efforts to improve education did not stop at improving public schools. Three programs are

More than 3,000 schools were built between 2000 and 2004, allowing 1.3 million new students to enter school.

aimed at helping teenagers and adults learn basic skills, stay in school, or go back to school. One program, Mission Robinson, targets older students who cannot read or write. Although most Venezuelan teenagers and young or middle-age adults can read and write today, many of the country's older citizens never learned

these basic skills. At Mission Robinson schools, volunteers teach basic reading, writing, and math during night classes.

Another type of school program, Mission Ribas, helps teenagers and adults graduate from high school by giving them a small grant of money. Mission Ribas classes are held during the day. Families that would have kept teenagers out of school for work can instead use the grant money to buy food and other necessities.

The last program, Mission Sucre, helps students pay for college. More than 100,000 Venezuelan students use this program to go to college each year.

Government Aids to Increase Literacy

In addition to strengthening public schools, the Venezuelan government supports other programs to increase literacy throughout the country. A system of nearly 700 public libraries offers access to books, computers, and the Internet. A government program has also given away millions of books, including nearly 1 million copies of the famous Miguel de Cervantes novel *Don Quixote.* For low-income Venezuelans, this program offers access to materials they need to learn to read.

Government programs under President Hugo Chavez have helped to decrease illiteracy throughout the country.

The literacy rate in 2006 was 93.4 percent, ranking Venezuela 39th in the world.

Nearly 1.5 million students have enrolled in the government's Mission Ribas program, which lets high school dropouts earn a diploma in half the time it usually takes.

Without it, most of them could not afford to go.

The three programs are named after key figures in Venezuela's battle for independence.

Mission Robinson is named after Simon Rodriguez who often used the pseudonym Samuel Robinson. He was private tutor to Simón Bolívar, one of Venezuela's greatest heroes. Bolívar led Venezuela's revolution against Spanish occupation in the early 1800s. Known as the Liberator, Bolívar also led the successful fight for the independence of Colombia, Peru, Ecuador, and Bolivia, which is named for him.

Mission Ribas is named after José Félix Ribas, a revolutionary and military leader. He was captured by the Spanish and executed in 1815.

Mission Sucre is named after Antonio José de Sucre, a revolutionary leader and a close friend and associate of Bolívar.

Traditional Venezuelan music and dance, played and performed throughout the country, is both preserved and modernized as teens take pride in their heritage.

2

From City Barrios to the Open Llanos

BY 2 P.M., MOST SCHOOLS IN CARACAS ARE OUT FOR THE DAY, AND STUDENTS BEGIN SPILLING OUT INTO THE BUSY CITY. Most schools don't have after school sports or arts programs, so teens head home to begin homework, chores, or private art classes. Some teens play baseball or soccer on a community team. The students weave in and out of crowds of pedestrians on the sidewalks, but they stay clear of the streets, which are clogged with noisy buses, cars, and motorcycles. The noise and pollution levels in this city of about 4 million people are extremely high. The streets are too busy for bicycles, so most teens walk or, if they have far to go and money for a ticket, hop on the subway that zooms underneath the city.

Inexpensive Gasoline

Although only about 30 percent of Venezuelans own cars, those who do tend to drive large luxury sedans or sport-utility vehicles. The government finances gasoline, so it costs about 429 bolívares (U.S.20 cents) a gallon. With little incentive for conserving fuel, Venezuelans tend to use plenty—resulting in particularly high levels of air pollution in the cities. In the 1980s, the government tried to curb pollution by limiting the days cars could be on the streets, according to their license plates. But wealthy Venezuelans simply bought an extra car so they could drive one every day of the week.

Even Venezuelans who don't own cars find ways to take advantage of cheap gas. Felix Mancilla, who sells pirated CDs and DVDs on the street in Caracas, uses gas to run a television and speakers for customers to test products. He pays just 4,292 bolívares (U.S.$2) a week to run the generator all day long. "Here, gasoline is cheaper than water," he says.

Many students are heading home to the city's *barrios*, neighborhoods where thousands of families have built one-room dwellings, called *ranchos*, out of brick, corrugated steel, clay, or concrete. Barrios line the hillsides in and around Caracas and other Venezuelan cities. Some people estimate that about half of the country's population resides in the barrios. Ramshackle concrete and wooden stairs connect zigzagging rows of ranchos throughout these neighborhoods. Unlike low-income housing in much of the rest of the world, Venezuela's barrios are not hidden at the edges of cities. They rise out of, and surround, most urban areas of the country. In Caracas, which lies in a valley surrounded by mountains, barrios fill every view of the city.

barrios
BAH-ree-ohs

ranchos
RAHN-chohs

Barrios are crowded and hard to keep clean. Often plumbing and electricity are not available, and crime and disease are major problems. But several government programs are aimed at improving life in the barrios. Residents can often receive building materials, electricity, water, and sewerage through the government. Large public housing units are being built to offer housing options. The government also has taken steps to improve rural life so people

Houses crowd a hillside in San Martin, a low-income residential area above Caracas.

will stay on farms rather than move to the crowded cities. In many rural areas, for example, the government has built paved roads, constructed schools and hospitals, and extended electrical service.

Teens who live in barrios might have chores or a job after school. Some take care of younger brothers and sisters. But many spend their afternoons the way teens across the world do—they

Health For All

For years, access to medical care was a major problem for all but the wealthiest Venezuelans. Diseases were common throughout the country, especially in the barrios and in rural areas. But in recent years, the government has begun providing health care services including checkups, medicine, and care for ill people. President Hugo Chavez told world leaders at the United Nations in September 2005, "Seventeen million Venezuelans—almost 70 percent of the population—are receiving, and for the first time, universal health care, including medicine. In a few years, all Venezuelans will have free access to an excellent health care service."

hang out with their friends. Outdoors, even in the narrow, twisted pathways of a barrio, teens usually play baseball. Sometimes sticks or broom handles substitute for a bat. Indoors, within some of the older ranchos—ones on which families have worked for years to make

Baseball is the most popular sport in Venezuela, and a number of Venezuelans have become top players in U.S. major league baseball.

them sturdy and waterproof—there's often a television.

Most teens from middle-income families—whose parents may be teachers, police officers, or small-business owners—head home to an apartment in one of Caracas' many steel and concrete high-rises. These teens usually have their own bedroom and sometimes their own bathroom. Their rooms vary greatly. Some are very simple, with just a bed, closet, and desk. Others are decorated to their own taste. This is where they will spend at least part of

Domestic service is one of the main occupations for low-income women in South America.

their afternoon, doing homework. Most likely, these families have household help, so teens don't have many chores in the afternoon. Many middle-income Venezuelan families hire women from nearby countries, such as Colombia, to clean and take care of the children.

The wealthiest Venezuelan families live in gated estates just outside the city. These homes are mansions and have beautiful gardens, swimming pools, and guards patrolling the property. Armed robbery is a danger in Venezuela, especially as transporting of illegal drugs brings more guns to the streets. Wealthy Venezuelan teens are not likely to be playing baseball in the street; they are more likely to spend afternoons inside their gated estates—an armed chauffeur may drive them to activities and friends' houses. These teens may also spend part of each year at their family's vacation home—a house along one of Venezuela's many beaches is common, as is an apartment in Miami or New York.

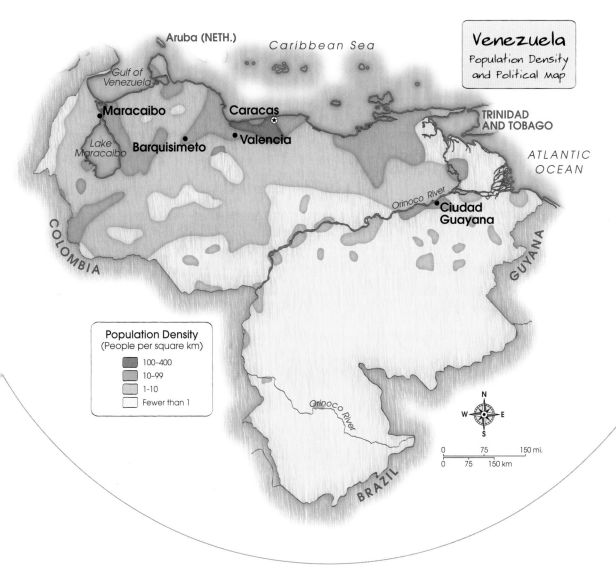

Venezuela
Population Density
and Political Map

Aruba (NETH.)

Caribbean Sea

Gulf of
Venezuela

Maracaibo

Caracas

TRINIDAD
AND TOBAGO

Lake
Maracaibo

Barquisimeto

Valencia

ATLANTIC
OCEAN

COLOMBIA

Orinoco River

Ciudad
Guayana

GUYANA

Population Density
(People per square km)

■ 100–400
■ 10–99
□ 1–10
□ Fewer than 1

Orinoco River

N
W   E
S

0   75   150 mi.
0   75   150 km

BRAZIL

Rural Life

Homes in rural Venezuela are different from city homes. About 85 percent of Venezuelans either live in cities along the Caribbean Sea or along the rivers that snake through the country. Only 15 percent of the population lives throughout the country's varied landscape of mountains, plains, and rain forests. And even though half of the country's land is south of the Orinoco River, only 5 percent of the people live there.

Along the Gulf of Venezuela, off of the Caribbean Sea, many families live in *palafitos*. They are houses built on stilts to keep water and insects out of them. Italian explorer and mapmaker Amerigo Vespucci saw them when he came to Venezuela in 1499. They reminded him of the city of Venice, Italy. On his map, he named the area Venezuela, "Little Venice." Many families still live in palafitos.

In the Amazon rain forest, members of the Yanomami tribe live together in a large round house made of wood and

palafitos
pah-lah-FEE-tos

Most palafitos are simple, with no running water or electricity.

thatch called a *yano*. Inside, each family has its own room for cooking over a fire and for sleeping. These living areas form a ring around a large open space in the middle of the yano, where the tribe meets and dances. Scientists estimate that there are about 15,000 Yanomami living in Venezuela today, and they consider the Yanomami to be the humans least touched by the modern world. Teens and other young members of the tribe do not go to school. Instead, they learn to gather and prepare food, to perform dances passed down from generation to generation, and to weave baskets.

Out on the *llanos*, the flat plains that lie between the Andes and the Orinoco River, the *llaneros* (cowboys), still live rough lives. When they are out on the range, they sleep outdoors with their cattle. These skilled horsemen are famous for riding

yano
YAH-noh

llanos
yah-nohs

llaneros
yah-NEH-ros

The Yanomami are believed to be the most primitive and culturally intact people in the world.

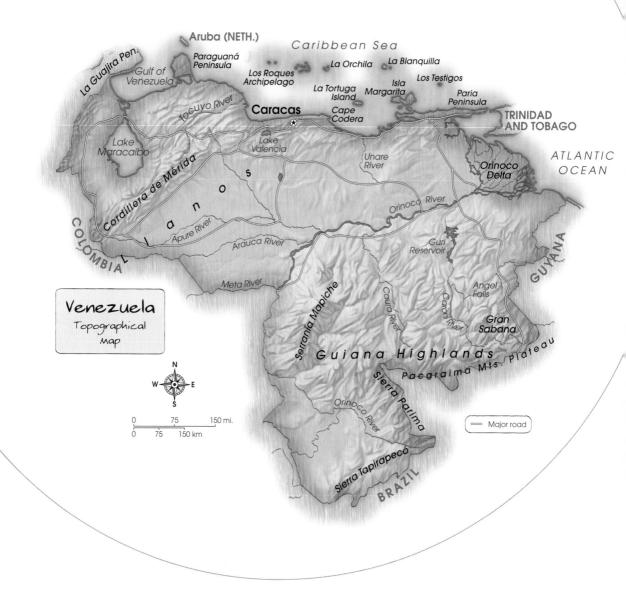

Venezuela
Topographical
Map

0   75   150 mi.
0   75   150 km

N
W · E
S

Major road

Aruba (NETH.)
Caribbean Sea
La Guajira Pen.
Paraguaná Peninsula
Gulf of Venezuela
Los Roques Archipelago
La Orchila
La Blanquilla
Los Testigos
Isla Margarita
La Tortuga Island
Paria Peninsula
Tocuyo River
Caracas
Cape Codera
TRINIDAD AND TOBAGO
ATLANTIC OCEAN
Lake Maracaibo
Lake Valencia
Unare River
Orinoco Delta
Cordillera de Mérida
L l a n o s
COLOMBIA
Apure River
Arauca River
Orinoco River
Guri Reservoir
GUYANA
Meta River
Serranía Mapiche
Caura River
Caroní River
Angel Falls
Gran Sabana
Guiana Highlands
Pacaraima Mts. Plateau
Orinoco River
Sierra Parima
Orinoco River
Sierra Tapirapecó
BRAZIL

and working barefooted. During the dry season, the llanos are blisteringly hot. But during the rainy season, the rivers flood the plains. Over the centuries, as llaneros rode through deep water all day, they found that it was better to ride barefooted than with wet socks and boots.

Today few teens live the nomadic llanero lifestyle. The teens who live on the plains are usually the children of plantation-owning ranchers. They often go to boarding schools or go live with relatives in a city so they can attend school for nine months of the year.

A llanero herds cattle on the llanos, in northwestern Venezuela.

During the summers, they learn about cattle ranching at home. Many teenage children of ranchers learn both the business and practical sides of ranching, so they can take over the family plantation.

The Andes mountain range stretches along the coast and the western part of Venezuela. Most of the country's major cities are located in the highlands—the lower peaks—of these mountains. A majority of the residents of smaller towns dotting the mountains have migrated to the cities, often to barrios. But some small towns remain, and residents there live much the way their ancestors did years ago: growing their own food, tending small herds of animals, and cooking and sleeping in small huts. These small towns near the Andes are known for their beauty, but most of all, they are known for their fresh produce and coffee.

Coffee, Anyone?

Before oil became the foundation of Venezuela's economy, the country depended on agriculture, particularly coffee and cocoa. Coffee plantations are located along the Andes Cordillera and Coastal Cordillera—mountainous areas in Venezuela. One of the most famous Venezuelan coffees—known as Maracaibo—is grown in the western part of the country near the Colombian border.

Coffee production also plays a social role in Venezuela. Since it is a traditional crop and is grown in the country, rural employment keeps some people from moving to urban areas.

Venezuelan coffees are different from other South American coffees. Their acidity levels are much lower, creating a smoother taste. Still, coffee production has declined because of price fluctuations and weather conditions, including torrential rain and floods.

Venezuela produces 800,000 to 1 million bags of coffee per year, but only a small number of these bags are exported. Most of the coffee is consumed by the Venezuelan people.

The arepa is Venezuela's most popular and traditional food.

Mealtime

Whether they live in the barrios, a gated estate, or on the llanos, families across Venezuela share many dining habits. Having eaten their largest meal in the early afternoon, most Venezuelans don't sit down to dinner until about 8 P.M., and when they do eat dinner, it is often a lighter snack of an arepa or leftovers from the midday meal.

Venezuelan food is influenced by the country's tropical climate and the people's mixed cultures. The lush mountains and rain forests yield plenty of

Selling fruit and vegetables is a common way for teens to make extra money for their families.

fresh fruits and vegetables. The coastal waters provide a bounty of seafood, and the plains produce some of the world's most renowned beef. Cooking styles reflect indigenous Indian traditions of stews and cornmeal breads, Caribbean and African mixtures of fruits and beans, and European recipes that contain meat, vegetables, and starches. Common ingredients include beef, pork, chicken, and fish, as well as many varieties of vegetables. Sweet fruits such as oranges,

melons, bananas, pineapples, guavas, tamarinds, and mangoes are eaten along with more savory foods such as potatoes and plantains.

The national dish of Venezuela is called *pabellón criollo*. It's made of shredded beef, black beans, and cheese, and served with fried plantains and rice. Bread made from a corn

pabellón criollo

pah-BAY-yahn cree-OH-yoh

batter is a staple of many favorite dishes, like the arepa. It is also used to make *cachapas*—thick, slightly sweet corn-cakes served with a mozzarella-type cheese—and empanadas. Arepas and empanadas are filled with beef, chicken, ham, sausage, fish, or cheese.

Venezuelan teens often drink sodas. Many popular American brands are available in both regular and diet—called "light" in Venezuela. Fruit-flavored carbonated soft drinks are also popular, including orange, apple, grape, and pineapple. For special occasions, teens enjoy traditional Venezuelan drinks like *batidos*, a thicker kind of fruit juice;

papelón con limón, a mixture of sugarcane juice and lemon; or fresh coconut milk. Coffee is the most common hot beverage, although Venezuelans also drink hot tea and chocolate drinks. Two of the most popular desserts are *palmeras*, candy-coated cookies shaped like palm trees, and *bombas*, sweet bread that is filled with cream.

cachapas

cah-CHAH-pahs

batidos

bah-TEE-dohs

papelón con limón

PAH-pay-lone cone lee-MONE

palmeras

palm-AIR-as

bombas

BOHM-bas

Venezuelan food, such as pabellón criollo, is a combination of African, European, indigenous, and Caribbean cuisine that has evolved over centuries.

In 2004, about 32 percent of households in Venezuela were nuclear, meaning both parents were present to care for children.

3 The Beauty of Family & Friends

BOTH BEAUTY AND GENEROSITY ARE REVERED IN VENEZUELAN SOCIETY. It is not unusual, or impolite, for men to comment on a woman's appearance, and spontaneous gifts are used to show affection. Venezuelans are known for being outgoing with everyone they meet.

This love of socializing may be one reason small neighborhood stores continue to flourish even as larger stores show up across Venezuelan cities. Each afternoon, the stores fill with people. The conversations often become very animated. Venezuelans tend to stand close together and gesture a lot with their hands during conversations. These actions are a way to simply be polite.

Mix of Cultures

Venezuela is a small country with a diverse population. With nearly 26 million people, the country's unique mix of cultures makes it hard to define a Venezuelan "look." Venezuelans may have black, brown, or blond hair. They may look African, Indian, or European. The largest group of Venezuelans is *mestizo* or *pardo*, meaning "mixed." These Venezuelans have mixed European and Indian ancestry. The next largest group is white, and they have mostly Spanish, Italian, and Portuguese ancestry. About 10 percent are black, with African and Caribbean ancestry, and the rest are full-blooded Native American Indian.

All of these ethnicities have contributed to Venezuela's unique culture, but the ethnic groups

mestizo
meh-STEE-zoh

pardo
PAR-doh

People in Venezuela

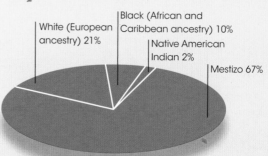

White (European ancestry) 21%

Black (African and Caribbean ancestry) 10%

Native American Indian 2%

Mestizo 67%

Source: United States Central Intelligence Agency. *The World Factbook—Venezuela.*

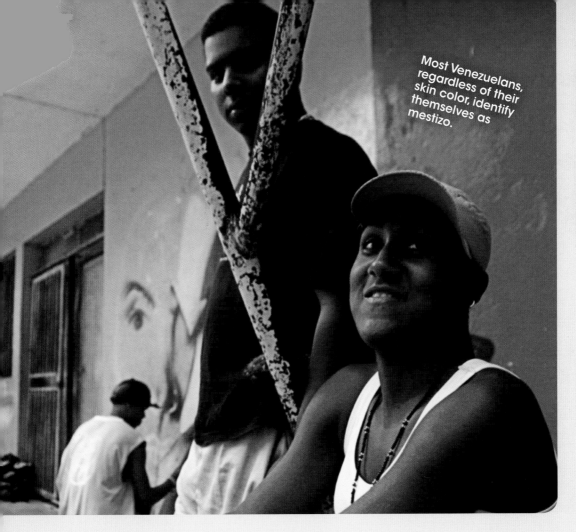

Most Venezuelans, regardless of their skin color, identify themselves as mestizo.

themselves do not tend to mix. Most city residents—as well as business and political leaders—are white or pardo. Blacks tend to live in smaller towns along the Caribbean coast, and native Indians live in the rain forests and interior of the country. As black and Indian Venezuelans have migrated to the cities, they have tended to live in barrios. Venezuelans define themselves by their ethnic background, and a strict ethnic hierarchy, or ranking, exists across the country. In this ranking, the "whiter" ethnicities are generally considered superior. Europeans are at the top of this social order, followed by pardos, blacks, and Indians. In general, Venezuelans marry within their social class or higher and do not want to marry people with skin darker than their own.

The average family in Venezuela has two or three children.

It's also a way to show affection. A greeting between old friends or strangers will likely include a kiss on each cheek, and while explaining something, Venezuelans may often touch their friends—even if they've just met—to emphasize a point.

Close Families

Venezuelans of all ethnic backgrounds share a respect for family. Although households tend to be small—most parents have two or three children—crowded gatherings are common. Parents usually live with only their children but grandparents often live close by. Venezuelan teens will most likely see their grandparents and several aunts, uncles, and cousins each day.

Family roles are clear and often quite traditional. Even though 31 percent of women work outside the home, they also remain in charge of child care and housekeeping. Mothers usually plan their children's schedules and take care of shopping and cooking responsibilities—either by doing these chores themselves or overseeing hired helpers who do them. If grandparents live nearby, they usually take care of younger children while the parents work. Food shopping is often part of the daily routine, with mothers or teenagers stopping at various stores—one for meat, another for fruits and vegetables—on their way home from work or school.

Gender defines children's roles, too. Parents tend to be more protective of girls than of boys. For instance, most parents always want to know where a teenage girl is, while boys have more freedom to come and go with their friends. In towns and cities, girls are usually given chores, such as cleaning and helping take care of younger siblings, while boys are asked to do manual labor, such as fixing things and performing outdoor tasks. By comparison, girls who live in the country are actually treated more like boys than city girls are. On a farm, everyone—boys, girls, men, and women—is expected to pitch in with whatever needs to be done.

Venezuelan fathers are responsible for providing for the family. Even when mothers work, fathers tend to earn more,

A common task on the farm is corralling the cattle.

45

and their jobs are considered more important. While mothers tend to the children's daily care, fathers usually make the household rules—and often these rules are quite strict. Most young people are allowed to socialize in groups, but they generally have to ask their parents before going out. Families usually have curfews, both for school nights and weekends, but the time of the curfew varies from family to family.

Most Venezuelan teens do not move out when they finish school. Instead, they live in their parents' home until their mid-20s, when most get married. When they do move to their

Young Venezuelans rely on their families for moral and economic support.

own home, it tends to be close to their parents and siblings.

Culture of Beauty

On a Saturday afternoon in Caracas, mothers and daughters flock to Centro Sambil, South America's largest shopping mall. With almost 550 stores, the five-level mall showcases fashions from Asia, Europe, and the United States.

Venezuelan culture places a high value on appearance, and shopping is a customary way for people to spend time together. Wealthy families shop at Caracas' expensive department stores, but they also schedule yearly or more frequent shopping trips to Europe and the United States. Even in lower-income families, a large portion of money is spent on fashion and beauty products.

With so many stores available, shopping plays a large role in Venezuelan life.

Beauty Pageants

A national fascination with beauty pageants is another reflection of Venezuelans' love of beauty. Across the country, young girls, teenagers, and young women participate in beauty pageants at a higher rate than citizens of almost any other country. In fact, Venezuela has produced more Miss World and Miss Universe winners than any other country. Several schools for training girls to compete in pageants exist in Caracas and other cities and towns. "These contests are the main way we show off our culture and beauty. That's why we start the girls at such a young age," explains Wilfredo Mendoza, president of Venezuela's Miss Teen Globe organization. "Pageants in Venezuela are like football in Brazil. In Brazil, they teach the kids to play football; here, the children learn about beauty contests."

Venezuelan women often claim top prizes in international beauty competitions.

Hanging Out & Keeping in Touch

Young Venezuelans are close to their families, and they form tight bonds of friendship with their peers as well. Teens have friends from school, sports, and other parts of their lives, and they get together frequently. Sometimes they go to movies, but most of the time they just hang out at someone's house or at the swimming pool or beach. Because the cities in Venezuela can be unsafe, especially at night, many parents prefer that their children have friends over or go to a friend's house. When they do go out, it is common for parents or hired drivers to chauffeur their children to and from evening events. This is due in part to safety concerns and also because the legal driving age in Venezuela is 18.

In their own homes, middle- and upper-income Venezuelan teens usually have no trouble keeping in touch with their friends. Almost one-third of all Venezuelans have cell phones, and 3 million are connected to the Internet.

In addition to spending time with friends, Venezuelan teens also date. Sometimes couples go out on their own, but more frequently they go with other friends to movies, restaurants, or nightclubs.

Friends often enjoy shopping together.

It can cost between 626,940 and 1,253,880 bolívares (U.S.$292 and $584) to participate in Carnival.

4 Dancing in the Streets

A WIDE AVENUE THROUGH DOWNTOWN CARACAS—usually jammed with cars and buses—is blocked off to traffic as teenagers, children, parents, and grandparents in wildly colorful costumes cheer and dance the joropo. The national dance features hand turns, waltz steps, and sweeping movements of the feet. A parade of elaborately decorated floats makes its way down the avenue, and the crowd rushes to gather candy and other trinkets being tossed by the float riders. It's Carnival, a two-day festival that takes place in February or March each year in Caracas and many other Venezuelan cities. Carnival is always the day before Ash Wednesday, the Christian holiday marking the beginning of the period of personal

joropo
yoh-ROW-poh

Venezuelans gather and pray at Saint Teresa Catholic church in Caracas during Holy Week, the week before Easter.

sacrifice leading up to Easter.

Venezuelan teens are used to celebrations involving family, food, and dancing. Holidays and celebrations are based on the European, African, and indigenous Indian backgrounds of Venezuelans. Many holidays are also steeped in Roman Catholic traditions. Even though fewer than half of Venezuelans attend church every week, 96 percent of the population consider themselves Catholic.

Semana Santa

Ash Wednesday, the day after Carnival, marks the beginning of Lent for Roman Catholics around the world. The 40 days of

Lent are a time of sobriety and sacrifice for Venezuelans and other Catholics. Some Venezuelans give up favorite foods such as chocolate or sweet drinks for those 40 days. Most Venezuelans usually have a vacation during Semana Santa, or Holy Week, the week before Easter. They go to church Monday, Thursday, and especially Good Friday. On Good Friday, there are solemn processions through villages and neighborhoods, leading to the church. They commemorate the crucifixion and death of Jesus Christ. The festivities end on Easter Sunday with Mass and other church and family events.

Nochebuena

Preparations for Nochebuena, or Christmas Eve, in Venezuela start on December 16—when families begin to decorate their homes with lights. Festivities do not end until January 6, on Día de Reyes, when Christians celebrate the three kings' visit to the baby Jesus. During the nine days before Christmas,

Holidays in Venezuela

Día de Año Nuevo (New Year's Day)—January 1
Día de Reyes (Day of the Kings/Epiphany)—January 6
Carnival—Monday and Tuesday before Ash Wednesday
Semana Santa (Holy Week)—from Palm Sunday to Easter
Día de San José (Saint Joseph's Day)—March 19
19 de Abril (19th of April)—April 19
Día del Trabajador (Labor Day)—May 1
Batalla de Carabobo (Battle of Carabobo)—June 24
5 de Julio (5th of July)—July 5
Natalicio del Libertador (Simón Bolívar's birthday)—July 24
Día de la Bandera (Flag Day)—August 3
Día de la Resistencia Indígena (Day of Indigenous Resistance)—October 12
Día de Todos los Santos (All Saints Day)—November 1
Inmaculada Concepción (Immaculate Conception)—December 8
Nochebuena (Christmas Eve)—December 24
Nochevieja (New Year's Eve)—December 31

Church officials carry a statue of the baby Jesus around a church after Christmas Mass in Caracas.

there are early morning church services, called *Misa de aguinaldos*. On Nochebuena, there is a midnight Mass celebrating the birth of Christ. There are often fireworks in the cities during the

Misa de aguinaldos
*MEE-sah day
ah-ghee-NAHL-dohs*

Christmas Flood

In December 1999, weeklong floods and mudslides ravaged Venezuela. Houses were either swept away by water or destroyed by mud, leaving 150,000 people homeless. Officials estimated the death count between 5,000 and 30,000. However, they were unable to come up with an accurate number, since many people were buried in their homes or carried away by the floods.

The number of missing people was even greater than the death toll. Survivors who were able to travel took refuge in nearby churches, schools, and stadiums, but many people were trapped in their homes. A few days before Christmas, Venezuelan President Hugo Chavez ordered military troops to go house to house in search of survivors. He also gave some soldiers an early Christmas leave to make room for thousands of homeless people at various military bases.

With the holiday season close at hand, Chavez asked that families open their homes to survivors during Christmas. As an example, Venezuelan first lady Marisabel Chavez opened the doors of the presidential residence for children orphaned by the disaster. With so many people reported missing, the government set up a Web site that allowed parents to post pictures of their lost children in the hope that someone would recognize them.

The flood in 1999 was Venezuela's worst natural disaster during the 20th century.

Christmas holidays.

Food is a very important part of Nochebuena festivities. The most traditional dish is *hallaca*. It is made from chopped beef, pork, and chicken with red peppers, onions, tomatoes, chickpeas, raisins, olives, and various herbs and spices, all mixed into a corn dough. The mixture is wrapped in plantain leaves and boiled.

hallaca
hah-YAH-cah

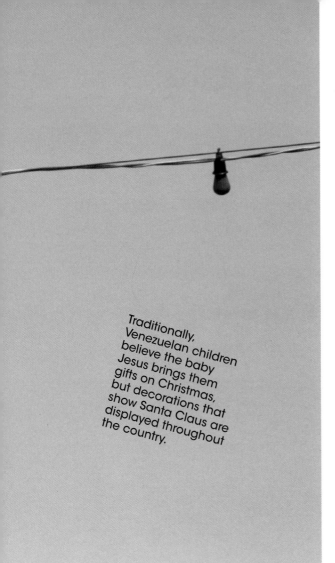

Traditionally, Venezuelan children believe the baby Jesus brings them gifts on Christmas, but decorations that show Santa Claus are displayed throughout the country.

for close family. They eat together and then go to Mass at midnight. At other times during the Christmas season, there are parties and visits with friends and relatives. On New Year's Day, the whole family gets together to celebrate.

Historical Celebrations

Venezuelans are proud to celebrate important nonreligious dates in their country's history. There are parades, fireworks, and speeches to mark many political anniversaries. On June 24, they celebrate Batalla de Carabobo, or the Battle of Carabobo, which took place in 1821. That battle helped Venezuelans win their fight for independence from Spain. Independence Day is celebrated on July 5, and Simón Bolívar's birthday on July 24.

Venezuela commemorates Día de la Resistencia Indígena, or Day of Indigenous Resistance, on October 12. On what was once celebrated as Columbus Day, it now commemorates the efforts by native people to resist Spanish colonization.

Children often get small gifts and candies at Nochebuena. They believe that baby Jesus left the gifts. Sometimes Venezuelan children get gifts on January 6, too. Those gifts are from the Three Wise Men who visited Jesus in the stable.

Nochebuena is usually a time just

In 2006, 52 percent of the workforce were freelancers, selling goods on the streets or from their homes.

5

Looking for Work

TEN VENEZUELAN TEENS WALK HOME FROM HIGH SCHOOL TOGETHER AND TALK ABOUT THEIR FUTURES IN THE WORKING WORLD. But out of this group, it's likely that one of them will not be able to find a job after graduating from high school or college. Across Venezuela, the unemployment rate has been on the rise for more than 10 years. In 2005, it was 12 percent, so for every 100 people looking for work, 12 could not find a job.

Of course, the high unemployment rate does not affect everybody equally. Teens who graduate from high school are more likely to find a job than those who don't, and college graduates are even more likely to find a job. And since teens who come from middle- or upper-income families are more likely to go to college, they are also more likely to find jobs. But even when they have a job, many Venezuelans find that they do not earn as much money as they need to support a family. For many years, wages have either stayed the same or fallen, while prices have risen. In 2005, the inflation rate—or the amount that prices rose on average—was 16 percent.

Unemployment Rates in Venezuela

The unemployment rate reflects the number of people who can't find work but are available to work and have taken steps to seek employment.

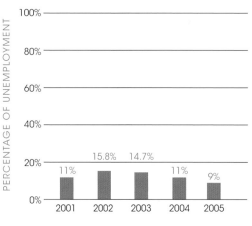

Source: LatinFocus Consensus Forecast.
Venezuela—Economic Indicators.

Teens & Money

Very few Venezuelan teens earn spending money from after-school jobs, and it's not just the high unemployment rate that stops them. Depending on where teens fit in to Venezuelan society, there are various reasons they don't work for spending money.

Teens who live in the barrios have probably experienced poverty their whole lives. They know their families struggle to buy food and other essentials, and they want to help however they can. If they can make extra money by doing odd jobs, then they often do them. But they don't keep the money they earn; it's used to help support the family. They also help at home with the same chores that some teens in other countries get paid to do—like washing, cooking, and taking care of younger siblings. But they don't earn money for those chores; they do them because they are expected to help out any way they can. They don't have extra money to spend, but neither do most of their friends. When they get together, they don't go out for fast food or to the movies. They play sports or just hang out.

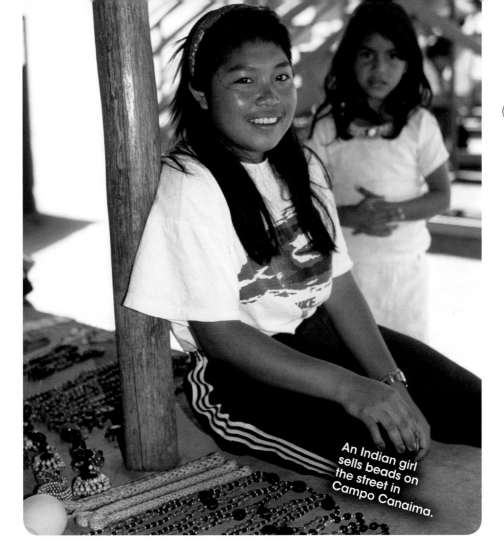

An Indian girl sells beads on the street in Campo Canaima.

Middle- and upper-income Venezuelan teens have the same financial needs as their peers around the world. They may have cell phone bills that can top 322,095 bolívares (U.S.$150) a month; they might want to stay on top of the latest fashions; or they may like to go to the movies with their friends. But most of them also don't earn spending money from after-school jobs. Their parents expect them to concentrate on school and usually give them an allowance for spending money. The amount varies widely—some get 5,000 to 10,000 bolívares (U.S.$2.33 to $4.66) a week, while others have credit cards with unlimited spending access. Sometimes older teenage boys take part-time jobs working in fast-food restaurants or helping to deliver mail, but teenage girls rarely have jobs. In such a patriarchal society, fathers feel they are not doing their job if they don't fully support their daughters.

First Jobs

Venezuelans begin their first jobs from age 14 to age 25, depending on when they leave school. The majority of jobs in Venezuela are in the services industry, which includes jobs such as driving taxis, serving food in a restaurant, and working in a hospital. Almost one-quarter of the country's jobs are in manufacturing—car factories, computer factories, and oil production. (Although the oil industry produces most of the money in the Venezuelan economy, it employs relatively few people.) The remainder of Venezuelans work on

Low wages and poor quality jobs force people to look for new ways to make money.

Division of Labor

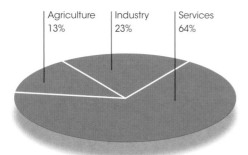

| Agriculture 13% | Industry 23% | Services 64% |

Source: United States Central Intelligence Agency. *The World Factbook—Venezuela.*

farms or in other agricultural jobs. But the type of job people have depends mostly on their level of education. The 20 percent of Venezuelan teens who leave school at age 14 are most likely to work on a farm if they live in the country or in

a series of low-paying jobs in a city. These teens are the most hurt by the high unemployment rate, because they haven't learned specific skills that would help them find jobs. They may work in a tire, paper, or cement factory. Or they may drive a taxi or sew clothes. Others will find jobs delivering packages and letters in the cities. Most companies hire motorcycle messengers since the

national postal service is slow and unreliable. Some teens will sell food and other items in marketplaces or as street vendors.

Students who graduate from a technical high school will have more options when they look for a job. They can work as nurses, medical technicians, electrical technicians, or computer programmers. Others may

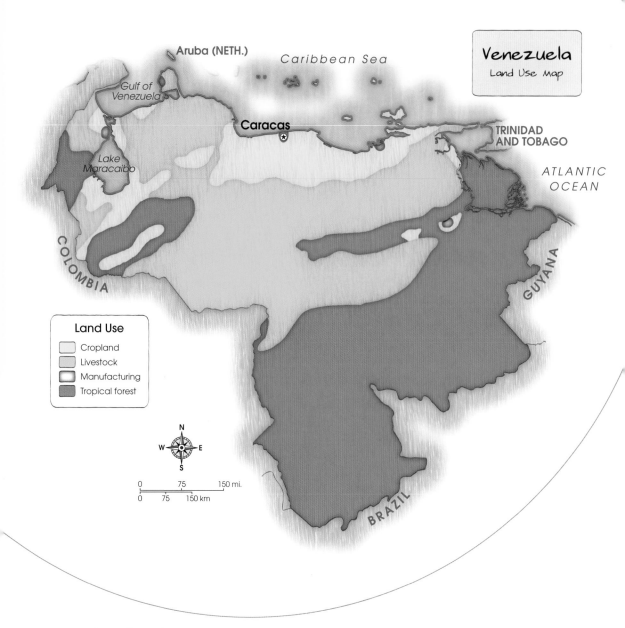

Venezuela
Land Use Map

Aruba (NETH.)

Caribbean Sea

Gulf of
Venezuela

Caracas

TRINIDAD
AND TOBAGO

Lake
Maracaibo

ATLANTIC
OCEAN

COLOMBIA

GUYANA

Land Use
- Cropland
- Livestock
- Manufacturing
- Tropical forest

N
W — E
S

0   75   150 mi.
0   75   150 km

BRAZIL

work in offices doing administrative work or data entry.

Most graduates from academic high schools go to college, but they may have to take a year or two off first.

Venezuela's universities are crowded and can only accept a limited number of students each year. Many students have to wait until there are openings available for them, and even then, they

Oil Industry

For the last 90 years, Venezuela's economy has focused on its oil production. In 1917, a large amount of oil was discovered in the Maracaibo Basin, triggering the country's oil industry. The oil industry thrived until 2002, when employees of the state-owned oil company—Petroleos de Venezuela (PdVSA)—went on strike. They opposed the ideas of President Chavez, who wanted total control over the PdVSA and its revenue. They hoped that they could force Chavez out of office by cutting off his access to the important industry. As a result,

Venezuela's economy weakened sharply since the country was unable to meet the demand for oil exports. The situation was so bad that it had to import oil from other countries. In response, Chavez dismissed 18,000 PdVSA workers—roughly half of the workforce—along with the management who were against him. He claimed they were mismanaging the company's revenue. Today the country's economy has almost fully recovered from the ordeal, and Venezuela has consistently been a top-10 supplier of oil to the United States, as well as a top-10 producer of crude oil. The Energy Information Administration states that Venezuela ranks eighth in oil exports, at 2.2 million barrels a day.

don't always get to study the subjects that most interest them. Sometimes this is because their first choice is not offered at the university near their home. But sometimes they are not able to get one of the limited spots in that program. Still, college graduates have by far the best job prospects in the country. They can find jobs as doctors, bankers, or lawyers. Science graduates can often find a high-paying job in the oil industry.

Cooperatives create jobs for workers. They also reduce the amount of food and other products that the country needs to import, decreasing Venezuela's dependency on the economies of other countries.

New Business Opportunities

The government is helping Venezuelans start businesses to improve life in villages, towns, and cities throughout the country. These programs, called cooperatives, are aimed at combating unemployment by providing opportunities for unskilled and inexperienced workers. Each cooperative can provide jobs for 200 people or more. In a cooperative, there's no boss: The members of the cooperative elect a

Cooperatives

Members of cooperatives work many hours and often do not make much money. For instance, Zaida Rosas, a grandmother who lives in a Caracas barrio, works in a textile cooperative with 200 other members. She works seven hours a day, five days a week, and earns a monthly income of 335,901 bolívares (U.S.$157)—even though Venezuela has a legal minimum wage of 539,739 bolívares (U.S.$252) per month. The members voted to pay themselves the lower salary "so we can pay back our loan," Rosas said. "We hope our working conditions will improve with time." Still, she said, she is glad for the cooperative experience. "My family is a lot happier—I've learned to write and have my third-grade certificate."

Venezuela's constitution requires the state to "promote and protect" cooperatives.

committee that makes all the decisions for the new business. They decide what the cooperative should make and sell. Then they take their plan to the government, which lends them the money to start the business. The government also provides training on how to run a cooperative, create business plans, and do accounting, as well as teaching basic skills such as reading and writing. Each member of the cooperative makes the same amount of money and works the same number of hours.

Cooperatives are exploding across Venezuela. In 2002, there were only about 2,000; in 2006, there were 108,000 cooperatives, with more than 1.5 million members, or workers. Cooperatives exist in all types of businesses, including clothing factories, cocoa processing plants, and taxi services. Many families' lives have been improved by cooperatives. Parents who could not find steady jobs have been able to develop skills and earn regular incomes to support their families. Many women work in cooperatives. Their children come to the cooperatives after school and do homework, play, or even help out. This way, the children can learn job skills as well.

Baseball became the country's most popular sport after Venezuela won the 1941 Amateur Baseball World Series in Havana, Cuba.

6

Always Time to Play Ball

IT'S EARLY MORNING, AND A BASEBALL FIELD IS EMPTY EXCEPT FOR FALLEN MANGOES SCATTERED ACROSS THE BASELINES. The field, in a small farming town west of Caracas, will soon be filled with boys working toward a dream of baseball stardom. The young Venezuelan teens who play here are already on their way to achieving their dream—they've been selected to train at one of Venezuela's many baseball academies. The academies are run by U.S. major league baseball teams as recruiting grounds for new talent.

Baseball is the national sport of Venezuela, and for many children from poor families, it is seen as an opportunity to escape poverty. More than 180

Venezuelans have played on U.S. major league teams, such as the Minnesota Twins and New York Yankees. Millions of Venezuelan boys dream of following in their heroes' footsteps and striking it rich in the big leagues. "For me, baseball has always been everything," said Pablo Morales, a 15-year-old pitcher. His friend, who is also 15 and plays catcher, adds: "Baseball is in my blood."

Each day, the boys spend hours practicing baseball and exercising. They also learn English and eat a balanced diet. One of the coaches explains:

It is believed that baseball was brought to Venezuela in the 1890s by students who had attended college in the United States.

"They run well, and they may have good bat speed. But some arrive here with nutrition problems and are really skinny. I also teach them to stay out of trouble, to do their job and to save their money. What I teach them here is for whatever career they end up having."

Although few of the teens at any academy will make the major leagues, some will undoubtedly end up playing in the U.S. minor leagues for a few years. The chance to achieve such a dream is the reason thousands of Venezuelan children—whether they

Venezuela's 72 islands and 1,750 miles(2,800 km) of coastline are popular vacation spots.

live in a barrio, on an estate, or on a farm—spend their free time playing baseball in the streets, the fields, or wherever they can.

Almost every neighborhood or small town has a baseball field, but it's not the only sport enjoyed by Venezuelan teens. Many play *fútbol* (soccer) as well. Higher-income Venezuelans also like to play tennis and golf.

fútbol
FOOWT-bowl

Sun & Water

Venezuela provides a natural playground for its teens: The sandy beaches along the Caribbean coast are a popular spot for hanging out with friends. Since the weather is almost always warm and sunny, a beach visit can be a daily activity for many teens.

On weekends, many teens pack up with their families to spend the day swimming and playing at a nearby beach. For a special trip, they might go to El Salto Angel, or Angel Falls. It is the tallest waterfall in the world. At a height of 3,212 feet (980 meters), it's taller than a 20-story building. Its longest free-fall drop is 2,648 feet (808 m).

Only higher-income families can afford to take vacations for a week or longer. They often go to Isla Margarita, a small island not far from Caracas where many upper-income families own beach houses. Middle-income families stay in hotels or rent beach houses.

The water of El Salto Angel drops more than twice the height of the Empire State Building and 15 times that of Niagra Falls.

75

Venezuelans love to watch fútbol on television.

The Small Screen

Despite the country's beautiful weather, Venezuelans don't spend all their time outdoors. Watching television is an indoor passion. Televisions are not very expensive to buy, and they are free to watch—even many barrio residents have TV sets. Most people keep their television on whenever they are home, to catch sports, news, or a favorite program. Since access to cable or satellite stations is expensive, many people

and bullfighting. Teenagers also watch reruns of American shows.

But the favorite shows are the *telenovelas* (television novels). These hour-long soap operas air six nights a week, beginning around 9 P.M. Each series plays for about six months, and then a new telenovela begins. Parents and teenagers often watch these shows together. The next day, talk on the bus, at the store, or on the street often centers on favorite characters and what will happen next.

telenovelas
tay-lay-noh-VAY-lahs

One television event is also very popular and takes place in the fall. Almost everyone watches the Miss Venezuela pageant every September.

The More the Merrier

Since most teens can't afford to go out to restaurants or nightclubs, they spend their free time at home with their family and friends. Venezuelans love to gather for eating, drinking, music, and dancing. It's not uncommon to have everyone from babies to grandparents at the same party.

Music and dancing are a part of almost every gathering. They dance salsa, merengue, and other dances, including the joropo, a dance for couples that varies slightly in different areas of the country. Traditional folk songs mix music from Europe

watch channels like Venevision and Radio Caracas Television, the two most popular national channels. Teens and families love to watch sports almost as much as they love to play them. They watch baseball, fútbol, horse racing,

Teens dance in a plaza in Mucuchíes, Venezuela.

and Africa. Venezuelan folk bands frequently use stringed instruments like *arpas*, or folk harps; *cuartos*, which are small and guitarlike; and *bandolas*, pear-shaped and also guitarlike. *Capachos*, or small maracas, are used as well. One of the most popular musical groups is Un Solo Pueblo, which means "one people."

arpas
AHR-pahs

cuartos
QUAHR-tohs

bandolas
BAHN-doh-lahs

capachos
cah-PAH-chose

Out on the Town

High up on the roof of Centro Sambil, Caracas' high-end shopping mall, teens are lined up to ride the roller coaster. Caracas teens with money to spend often pass afternoons or entire weekend days at this rooftop amusement park. The enormous shopping mall also features a bowling alley, movie theaters, and an aquarium.

Los Amigos Invisibles

In 1991, six friends in Caracas decided to form a Latin dance band that combined contemporary Latin dance music with a variety of other music, including jazz, disco, and funk. They named the band Los Amigos Invisibles and began performing at nightclubs in Caracas. A few years later, with financial help from a few friends, they released their debut album, *A Typical and Autoctonal Venezuelan Dance Band*. After a rough start and some tough breaks, the band recorded its second album, entitled *The New Sound of the Venezuelan Gozadera*. The

members of the band quickly found themselves on tour, and they were unable to spend time creating new music. After three years, they released *Arepa 3000: A Venezuelan Journey into Space*, an album that would land the band nominations in the 2000 Grammy awards and 2000 Latin Grammy awards. Thriving on the success of its nominations for music awards, the band produced many more CDs in the following years. They have toured the United States, Europe, Mexico, and South America, and the band appeared on *The Jimmy Kimmel Show* in 2005. The band's members stress that they are making music that challenges them and allows them to have fun.

Los Amigos Invisibles performed at the 2006 Bang Music Festival in Miami, Florida.

Most Venezuelans don't have the money required to shop here, but those who do have money keep the 550 stores busy daily from 10 A.M. to 9 P.M.—unusually long hours in a country that customarily closes down over lunchtime. In fact, opening-day crowds in 1999 were so overwhelming that the new escalators broke down under the strain of all the people.

This example of luxury is located within miles—and view—of most of Caracas' poverty-stricken barrios. It represents the always-present contrast between the wealthy and the poor in Venezuela. And it also reflects the Venezuelan people's love of beauty, image, and money. During the oil-boom years of the 1970s and 1980s, wealthy Venezuelans became used to buying

...Un Corolla!

MERCANTIL

The Centro Sambil is the largest shopping mall in South America.

LANCÔME

hypnôse

Louis Vuitton is only one of many popular stores in the Centro Sambil.

everything they wanted. Without luxury shopping centers in Venezuela, they headed to Miami or New York for weekend shopping sprees. When oil money dried up in the 1990s, Venezuelans' appetite for luxury did not. Since 1999, crowds have flocked to the Centro Sambil mall, and similar shopping centers have sprung up in other Venezuelan cities. There is now a Centro Sambil in Maracaibo, a city in the western Zulia state where most Venezuelan oil comes from.

But even Venezuelan teens who can't afford luxury find ways to shop and go to the movies. American and European fashions are popular, and cheaper versions of brand-name clothes can often be bought at street markets. Venezuelans love to dress up, and while teens will usually wear jeans and T-shirts, they almost never wear athletic clothing like sweat suits unless they are playing sports. Teens without much money can also get their fix of American movies and movie stars by going to the theater on Mondays and Thursdays, when many shows are half price.

Looking Ahead

TODAY VENEZUELA REMAINS A COUNTRY OF DIFFERENCES.
Its diverse population has drawn from combined South American, European, and African influences to create a unique Venezuelan culture. Its people are known for their generosity and friendliness, and they have learned to make the most of their country's rich resources, including oil and fertile crop-growing land. Venezuelans continue to confront the issues of poverty, unemployment, and pollution. But government programs are working to improve education, create jobs, and improve the environment.

Venezuelan teens surround themselves with friends and family and focus on school, work, and the future. They enjoy their country's natural beauty and will one day figure out how to make their own contributions to improving life in their homeland. And they will have plenty of company—the average age in Venezuela is just 26. This large young generation holds the key to the country's future.

At a Glance

Official name: Bolivarian Republic of Venezuela

Capital: Caracas

People

Population: 25,730,435

Population by age group:
0–14 years: 29.1%
15–64 years: 65.7%
65 years and over: 5.2%

Life expectancy at birth: 74.54 years

Official language: Spanish

Other languages: Numerous indigenous dialects

Religions:
Roman Catholic: 96%
Protestant: 2%
Other: 2%

Legal ages:
Alcohol consumption: 18
Driver's license: 18
Employment: 14
Marriage: 14 for females, 16 for males (though exceptions are made)
Military service: 18
Voting: 18

Government

Type of government: Federal republic

Chief of state and head of government: President, elected by popular vote

Lawmaking body: Asamblea Nacional, (Unicameral National Assembly), with 167 seats; members elected by popular vote to serve five-year terms

Administrative divisions: 23 states, one capital district, and one federal dependency.

Independence: July 5, 1821 (from Spain)

National holiday: Independence Day, July 5

National symbols: The national emblem features eight stars that stand for the eight initial provinces.

Geography

Climate: Tropical; hot and humid with more moderate temperatures in the highlands

Total area: 364,820 square miles (948,532 square kilometers)

Major landforms: Andes mountains, Maracaibo Lowlands, central plains (llanos), Guiana Highlands

Major rivers: Orinoco, Caroní, Apure

Highest point: Pico Bolívar, 16,437 feet (5,013 meters)

Lowest point: Caribbean Sea, sea level

Economy

Currency: Venezuelan bolívar

Population below poverty line: 47%

Major natural resources: Petroleum, natural gas, coal, iron ore, gold, diamonds, bauxite, other minerals, hydroelectric power

Major agricultural products: Corn, sorghum, sugarcane, rice, bananas, vegetables, coffee, beef, pork, milk, eggs, fish

Major exports: Oil, steel, aluminum, textiles, apparel, rice, cigarettes, fish, tropical fruits, coffee, cocoa

Major imports: Raw materials, machinery and equipment, transportation equipment, construction materials, agricultural goods

Historical Timeline

 Inca civilization flourishes in South America

Dictator Juan Vicente Gomez governs at a time when Venezuela becomes the world's largest exporter of oil

 British colonies in North America declare their independence from Great Britain

Simón Bolívar and his troops defeat Spanish troops at the Battle of Carabobo; Bolívar establishes the Republic of Gran Colombia, which begins to break apart in 1829 into the countries of Venezuela, Colombia, and Ecuador

| **2000** B.C. | A.D. C.**1000** | **1498–1499** | **1749** | **1776** | **1810** | **1821** | **1908–1935** |

Three main tribes, the Carib, Arawak, and Chibcha, populate the area that becomes Venezuela

First rebellion against Spanish colonial rule

Venezuelan patriots take advantage of Napoléon Bonaparte's invasion of Spain to declare independence; the Independence Act is signed in 1811

Christopher Columbus and Alonso de Ojeda visit Venezuela; Spanish settlement begins in 1521

 Historical World Event

The oil boom boosts
Venezuela's economy

 The Korean War

Venezuela's first
presidential handover
from one civilian to
another takes place
when Raul Leoni is
elected president

Jimenez is ousted;
Democratic Action Party
wins presidential election

| 1939–1945 | 1947–1948 | 1950–1953 | 1958 | 1960 | 1964 | 1969 | 1973 |

 World War II

The first democratically
elected ruler is overthrown
within eight months in
a military coup led by
Marcos Perez Jimenez

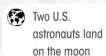 Two U.S.
astronauts land
on the moon

Venezuela joins with
Iran, Iraq, Kuwait, and
Saudi Arabia to form the
Organization of Petroleum
Exporting Countries

Historical Timeline

An economic depression causes riots, martial law, and a general strike

 Terrorist attacks on the two World Trade Center Towers in New York City and on the Pentagon in Washington, D.C., leave thousands dead

Chavez wins a third term, vowing to boost social programs

Hugo Chavez is swept into office promising "revolutionary" social policies; he wins again in 2000

1983–1984   **1989**   **1991**   **1998**   **1999**   **2001**   **2002**   **2006**

Soviet Union collapses

A nine-week strike in the oil industry causes fuel shortages

Fall in world oil prices generates unrest and cuts in welfare spending

Severe floods and mudslides hit the north, killing tens of thousands of people

Glossary

academic	form of schooling in which students learn information rather than hands-on skills
biology	the study of plant and animal life
curfews	set times to be home, usually for a young person
illiteracy	inability to read or write
indigenous	native to a place
literacy rate	the percentage of the population 15 years and older who can read and write
literate	able to read and write
plantain	starchy banana-like fruit, which is always eaten cooked
patriarchal	of or relating to the oldest member or representative of a group
scholarships	money given to students to pay for school
tuition	money paid for schooling

Additional Resources

IN THE LIBRARY

Aalgaard, Wendy. *Venezuela in Pictures*. Minneapolis: Lerner Publications, 2005.

Crooker, Richard A. *Venezuela*. New York: Chelsea House Publishers, 2006.

Ng, Yumi. *Welcome to Venezuela*. Milwaukee: Gareth Stevens Publishing, 2004.

Winter, Jane Kohen, and Kitt Baguley. *Venezuela*. New York: Benchmark Books, 2002.

ON THE WEB

For more information on this topic, use FactHound.

1. Go to www.facthound.com
2. Type in this book ID: 0756524474
3. Click on the *Fetch It* button.

FURTHER READING

Look for more Global Connections books.

Teens in Australia   *Teens in Kenya*
Teens in Brazil   *Teens in Mexico*
Teens in China   *Teens in Russia*
Teens in France   *Teens in Saudi Arabia*
Teens in India   *Teens in Spain*
Teens in Israel   *Teens in Vietnam*
Teens in Japan

Source Notes

Page 26, sidebar, line 27: Mike Ceaser. "Life in the Land Where Filling up an SUV Costs $3." *The Christian Science Monitor.* 28 Sept. 2005. 22 Nov. 2006. www.csmonitor. com/2005/0928/p04s01-woam.html

Page 28, sidebar, line 14: Bob Briton. "Venezuela and the Century of Socialism." *Political Affairs.net.* January 2006. 22 Nov. 2006. www.politicalaffairs. net/article/view/3260/1/162/

Page 43, column two, line 7: Marriage, Family and Kinship. *Countries and Their Cultures.* Thomson Gale, 2005. 12 Dec. 2006. www.everyculture.com/To-Z/ Venezuela.html

Page 48, sidebar, column two, line 5: David Rochkind. "Girls' World." *The (London) Independent.* 6 Nov. 2004. 22 Nov. 2006. www.findarticles. com/p/articles/mi_qn4158/is_20041106/ai_n12818036

Page 68, sidebar, line 16: Betsey Bowman and Bob Stone. "Venezuela's Cooperative Revolution: An Economic Experiment is the Hidden Story Behind Chávez's Bolivarian Revolution." *Dollars and Sense.* July/ August 2006. 22 Nov. 2006. www.dollarsandsense.org/archives/2006/ 0706bowmanstone.html

Page 72, column 1, line 6: John Otis. "Baseball a Way Out for Teens of Venezuela." *Houston Chronicle.* 19 June 1998. 22 Nov. 2006. www.chron.com/content/chronicle/world/98/06/20/venezuela.2-0.html

Page 72, column 2, line 3: Ibid.

Page 73, column 1, line 1: Ibid.

Pages 84–85, At a Glance: United States. Central Intelligence Agency. *The World Factbook—Venezuela.* 30 Nov. 2006. 6 Dec. 2006. www.cia.gov/cia/publications/factbook/geos/ve.html

Select Bibliography

Bowman, Betsy, and Bob Stone. "Venezuela's Cooperative Revolution: An Economic Experiment is the Hidden Story Behind Chávez's Bolivarian Revolution." *Dollars & Sense.* July/August 2006. 6 Dec. 2006. www.dollarsandsense.org/archives/2006/0706bowmanstone.html

Brosnan, Greg. "Venezuela 'Revolution' Gets a Hip-hop Beat." *Reuters.* 23 May 2006. 6 Dec. 2006. www.globalexchange.org/countries/americas/venezuela/3942.html

Ceaser, Mike. "Life in the Land Where Filling Up an SUV Costs $3." *The Christian Science Monitor.* 28 Sept. 2005. 6 Dec. 2006. www.csmonitor.com/2005/0928/p04s01-woam.html

Egan, Bill. "Christmas in Venezuela." 12 May 2006. www.christmas.com/worldview/ve

Ellner, Steve, and Daniel Hellinger (eds). *Venezuelan Politics in the Chavez Era: Class, Polarization & Conflict.* Boulder, Colo.: Lynne Rienner Publishers, 2003.

Espada, Carolina. "Caracas Local Custom Tips." *Virtual Tourist.com.* 24 Aug. 2006. 18 May 2006. www.virtualtourist.com/travel/South_America/Venezuela/Distrito_Federal/Caracas-1637665/Local_Customs-Caracas-Cultural_Tips-R-1.html

Euromonitor. "Consumer Lifestyles in Venezuela." February 2003. 18 May 2006. www.euromonitor.com/pdf/conlife-venezuela.pdf

Ferguson, James. *Venezuela: A Guide to the People, Politics, and Culture.* London: The Latin America Bureau, 1994.

"Focus On VENEZUELA School Program." American Field Service (AFS*).* 7 May 2006. www.afs.ch/f/pdf/FP_SIA/SIA_YP_Venezuela.pdf

"Food and Drink." Thinkvenezuela.net. 10 May 2006. www.thinkvenezuela.net/english/venezuela_general_information.htm

Gordon, Raymond G., Jr. (ed.) *Ethnologue: Languages of the World.* 15th ed. Dallas: SIL International, 2005. 5 May 2006. www.ethnologue.com/

Gould, Jens Erik. "With Oil's Cash, Venezuelans Consume." *New York Times.* 8 June 2006, p. C1.

Guss, David M. *The Festive State: Race, Ethnicity and Nationalism as Cultural Performance*. Berkeley: University of California Press, 2000.

Haggerty, Richard A. *Venezuela: A Country Study*. 4th ed. Washington: Federal Research Division, Library of Congress, 1993.

Hoag, Christina. "Retail Revolutionary: How Does a Real Estate Developer Become a Household Name?" *Latin CEO: Executive Strategies for the Americas*, March 2001. 6 Dec. 2006. www.findarticles.com/p/articles/mi_m0OQC/is_3_2/ai_100508533

Landino, Leonte A. "The Road to the Big Leagues." *Baseball Around the World: Venezuela*. 2002. 16 May 2006. http://iml.jou.ufl.edu/projects/Fall02/Landino/journeyframeset.html

Otis, John. "Baseball a Way Out for Teens of Venezuela." *Houston Chronicle*, 19 June 1998. 10 Aug. 2006. www.chron.com/content/chronicle/world/98/06/20/venezuela.2-0.html

Rimmer, Louise. "The Threatened Forest People Who Are Learning the Language of Survival." *The Independent*. 6 Dec. 2003. 15 June 2006. http://news.independent.co.uk/world/americas/article81408.ece

Romero, Simon. "For Venezuela, As Distaste for U.S. Grows, So Does Trade." *New York Times*. 16 Aug. 2006. www.nytimes.com

Steen, Mary. "Venezuela: A Cultural Profile." Published by Anti-Racism, Multiculturalism and Native Issues (AMNI) Centre, Faculty of Social Work, University of Toronto, 2000. 14 May 2006. www.cp-pc.ca/english/venezuela/venezuela_eng.pdf

Monitoring Report. Executive Office, Education Sector UNESCO. 1 April 2005. 4 May 2006. http://unesdoc.unesco.org/images/0014/001462/146204e.pdf

United States. Central Intelligence Agency. *World Factbook: Venezuela*. 15 June 2006. 11 July 2006. https://www.cia.gov/cia/publications/factbook/geos/ve.html

United States. Department of State, Bureau of Western Hemisphere Affairs. "Background Note: Venezuela." March 2006. 10 May 2006. www.state.gov/r/pa/ei/bgn/35766.htm

"Venezuela." *Worldatlas.com*. 15 June 2006. http://worldatlas.com/webimage/countrys/samerica/ve.htm

Embassy of the Bolivarian Republic of Venezuela in the United States of America. 6 Dec. 2006. www.embavenez-us.org/

"Venezuela's Literacy Triumph." Venezuela Information Office. 9 May 2006. www.rethinkvenezuela.com/downloads/literacy.htm

Wagner, Sarah. "Venezuela: Illiteracy Free Territory." Non Aligned Press Network. 22 April 2005. 14 May 2006. www.voltairenet.org/article124841.html

World Bank Group. GenderStats: Venezuela, 2004. 15 June 2006. http://devdata.worldbank.org/genderstats/genderRpt.asp?rpt=profile&cty=VEN,Venezuela&hm=home

Index

About the Author
Sandy Donovan

Sandy Donovan has written several books for young readers about history, economics, government, and other topics. She has also worked as a newspaper reporter, a magazine editor, and a Web site developer. She has a bachelor's degree in journalism and a master's degree in public policy, and lives in Minneapolis, Minnesota, with her husband and two sons.

About the Author
Caryn Gracey Jones

Caryn Gracey Jones is a freelance writer. She and her husband live in Denver, Colorado. Caryn worked in children's publishing, including at Compass Point Books, for nearly five years. She has also worked in several nonprofit organizations, including the Children's Museum of Denver, March of Dimes of southeast Wisconsin, and Mile High United Way. She has a bachelor's degree in journalism from Marquette University and is working on her master's degree in writing from De Paul University.

About the Content Adviser
Ines Rojas

Our content adviser Ines Rojas is an assistant professor in the School of Modern Languages at the Universidad de Los Andes in Venezuela. She is a professor of English grammar and international relations, and her current research interests include women's political participation in Latin America.

Image Credits